RSITY OF   LIB/LEND/002

TOPIC BOX

My Body

Brian Moses

Wayland

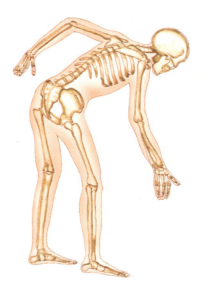

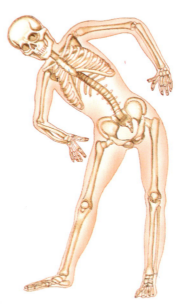

Titles in this series
Castles
Dinosaurs
Fairs and Circuses
Houses and Homes
Minibeasts
My Body
The Seasons
Transport

This book was prepared for Wayland (Publishers) Ltd
by Globe Education, Nantwich, Cheshire

Design by Pinpoint
Artwork by Peter Bull

First published in 1995 by
Wayland (Publishers) Ltd
61 Western Road, Hove
East Sussex BN3 1JD

Printed and bound in Italy by
L.E.G.O. S.p.A., Vicenza

British Library Cataloguing in Publication Data

Moses, Brian
My Body. – (Topic Box Series)
I. Title II. Series
612

ISBN 0 7502 1241 1

Picture acknowledgements
APM Studios cover, 3t, 3b, 4, 7, 10;
Martyn Chillmaid 28, 29tl, 29tb, 29r;
Science Photo Library (Van Bucher) 5, (Claude Nuridsany/Marie Perennou) 8, (Doug Plummer) 11, (Larry Mulse
(Will & Deni McIntyre) 14t, (Custom Medical Stock Photo) 18l, (Adam Hart-Davis) 18r, (Jerry Wachter) 20, (Oscar
Tony Stone (Jo Browne/Mick Smee) 1 and 14, 9, (Elan Sun Star) 15, (David Madison) 16 and 22t, (Matthew McV
(Lori Adamski Peek) 26

Contents

Bones

There are many hard bones inside your body that allow you to stand up straight and to move about.

These bones also protect the soft areas inside you. Your heart and lungs are safe inside your rib cage. Your brain is protected by your hard skull.

As you grow older, your bones grow and change shape until you are an adult. If you break a bone it will grow until the break is healed.

Gently press different parts of your body and feel the bones beneath your skin.

This X-ray photograph shows the bones of the spine and the ribs. The dark areas show the lungs.

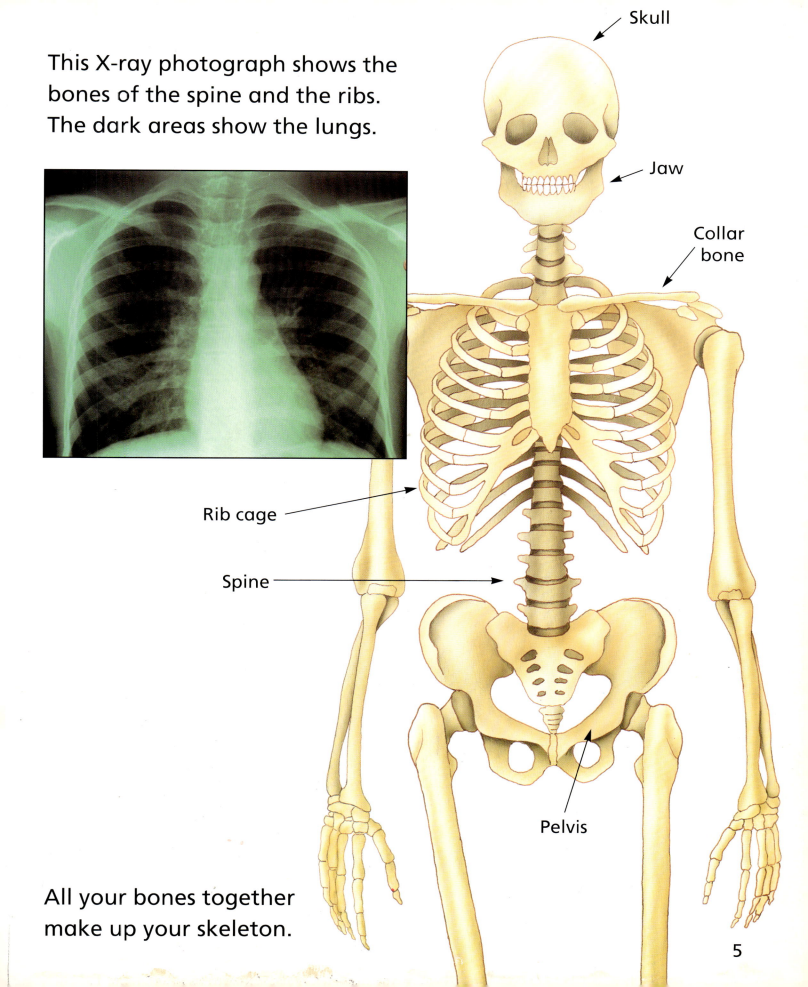

Skull

Jaw

Collar bone

Rib cage

Spine

Pelvis

All your bones together make up your skeleton.

5

Joints

The places where your bones link together are called joints. Two types of joints that you have are hinge joints and ball-and-socket joints.

All joints have pads of cartilage that stop the bones from wearing out.

Your joints move because you have muscles connecting the bones together. Muscles need exercise to keep them working properly.

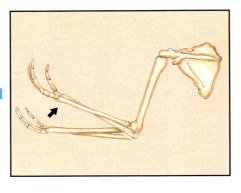

Hinge joints move in only one direction.

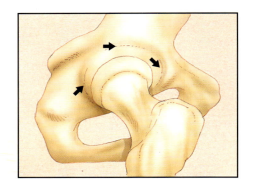

Ball-and-socket joints can swivel in more than one direction.

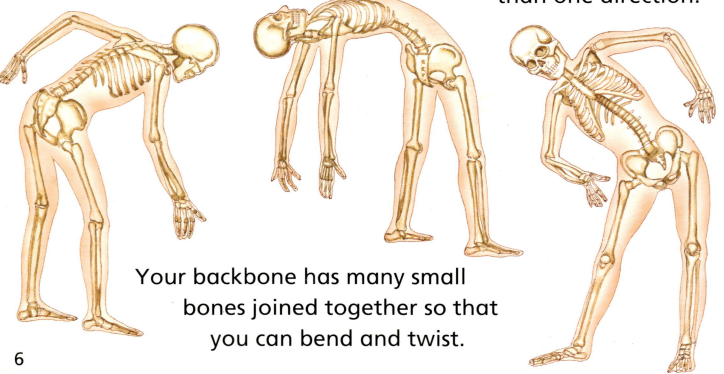

Your backbone has many small bones joined together so that you can bend and twist.

Exercise keeps your joints
and muscles healthy.
It also helps you to relax.

Cells

Your body is made up of millions of cells. These cells are so tiny that you need a powerful microscope to see them.

Different kinds of cells do different jobs. Muscle cells allow you to stretch and squeeze. Nerve cells carry messages between your brain and every other part of your body.

Cells can divide into two or change from one kind to another. This is how your body grows.

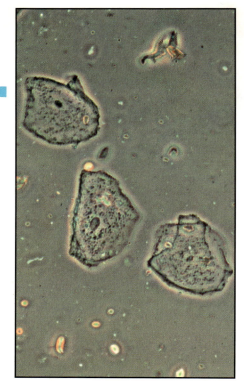

(Above) Cells taken from the inside of a human mouth and magnified by a microscope.

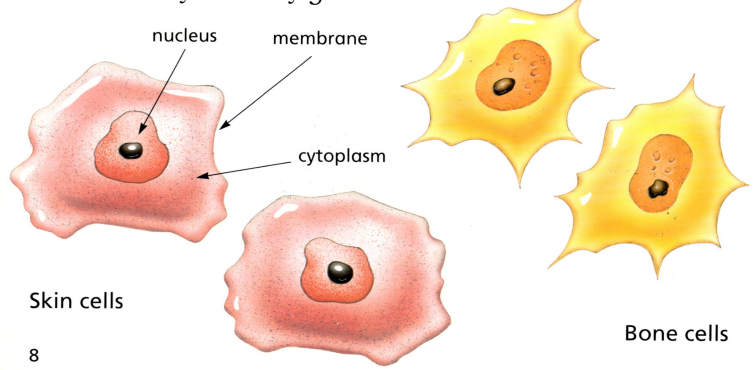

nucleus

membrane

cytoplasm

Skin cells

Bone cells

8

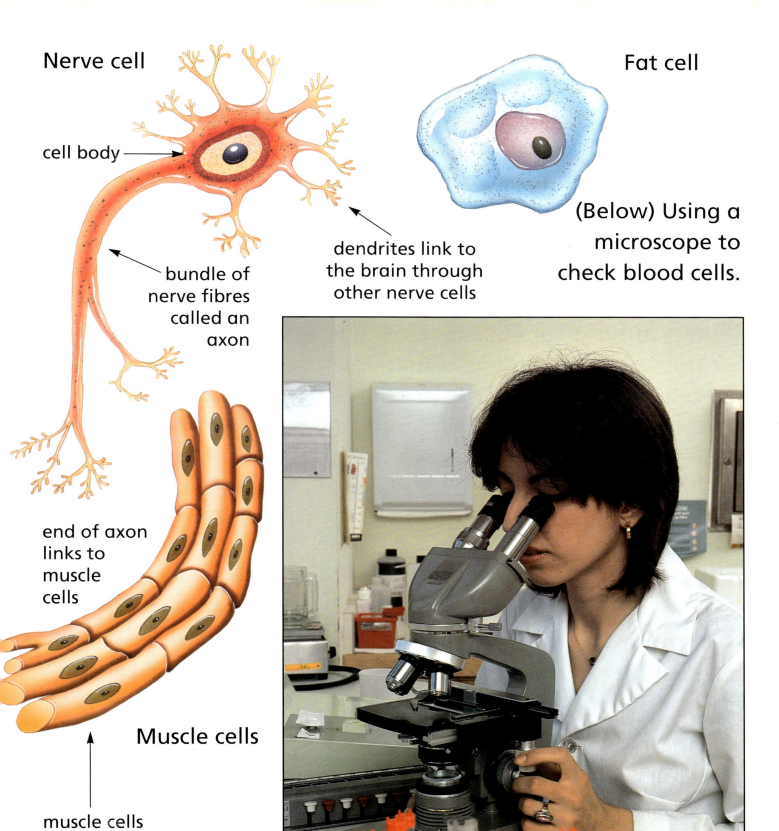

Nerve cell

Fat cell

cell body

dendrites link to
the brain through
other nerve cells

(Below) Using a
microscope to
check blood cells.

bundle of
nerve fibres
called an
axon

end of axon
links to
muscle
cells

Muscle cells

muscle cells
form fibres
that stretch
and contract

9

Your Heart

Your heart is a strong muscle that pumps your blood around your body. Your heart beats each time it pumps.

The pumping squeezes your blood through the heart and into your arteries. At the same time, it sucks blood back from the rest of your body to your heart through the veins.

The movement of the blood around your body is called your circulation.

If you are a 7-year old child, your heart pumps about 90 times each minute.

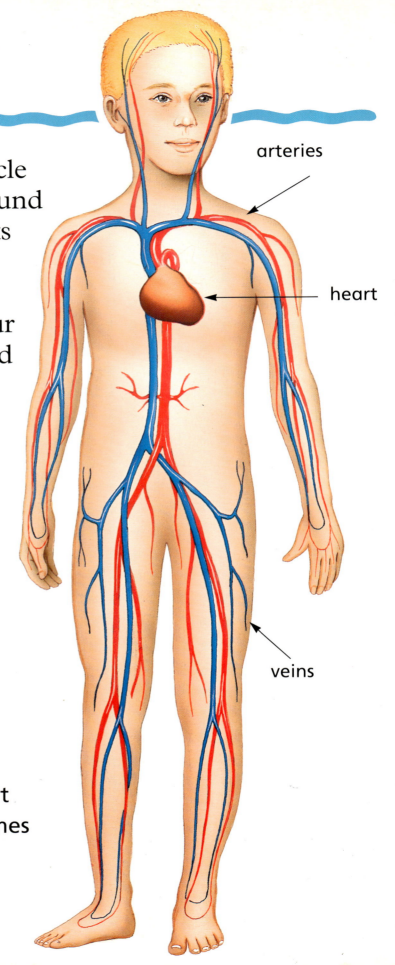

arteries

heart

veins

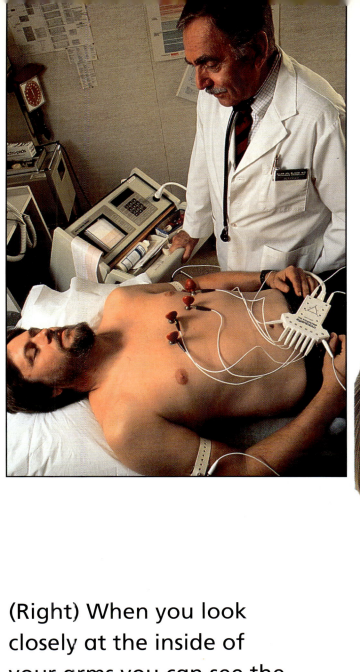

(Left) Doctors have machines that can check on your heart beat.

(Right) When you look closely at the inside of your arms you can see the blue veins under your skin.

What is Blood?

Your blood carries food and oxygen to every part of your body.

It has many cells doing different jobs. Red cells carry oxygen, white cells fight germs and platelets stop you bleeding when you cut yourself.

Not all blood is the same. You may have a different type of blood from your friends. There are four blood groups called A, B, AB and O.

Platelets mend any holes or tears in your veins and arteries.

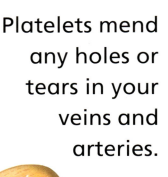

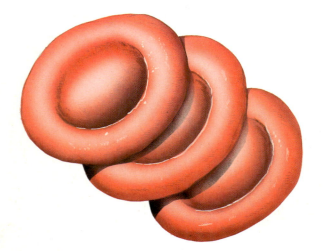

Red blood cells carry oxygen.

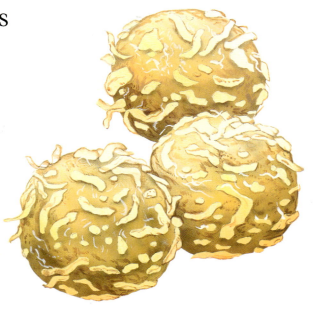

White blood cells fight germs.

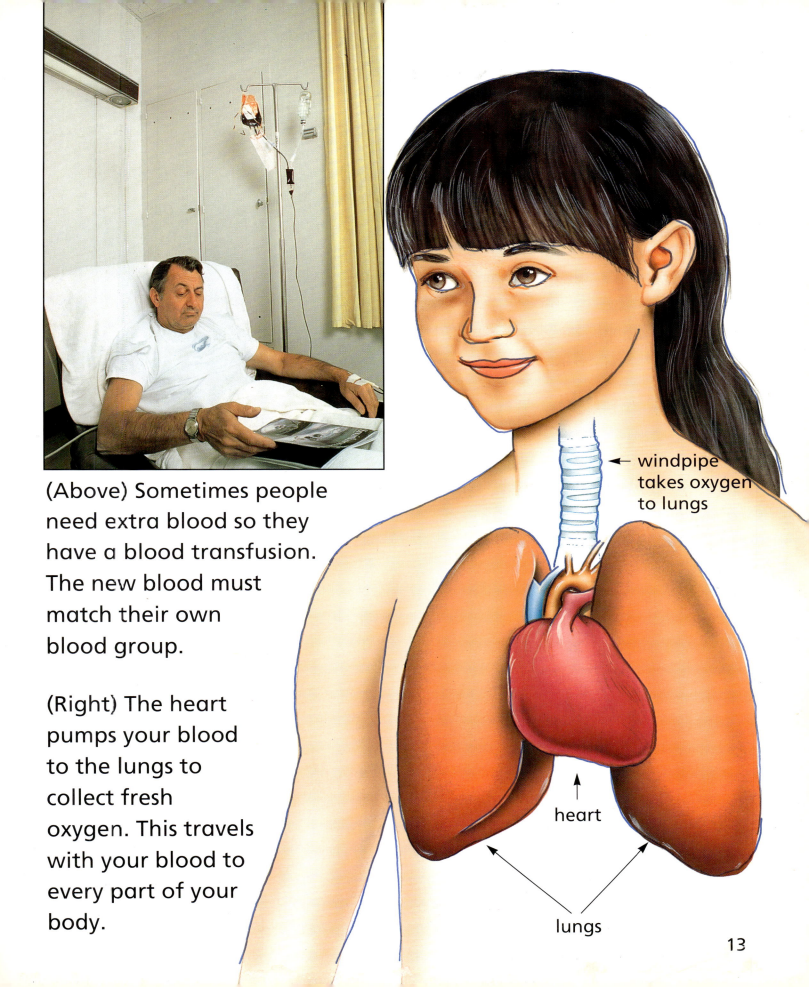

(Above) Sometimes people need extra blood so they have a blood transfusion. The new blood must match their own blood group.

(Right) The heart pumps your blood to the lungs to collect fresh oxygen. This travels with your blood to every part of your body.

windpipe takes oxygen to lungs

heart

lungs

13

Skin

Your skin covers the outside of your body. It stops water and germs getting in and it stops your blood leaking out.

It gets its colour from a substance called melanin. Dark-skinned people have lots of melanin. Light-skinned people have very little melanin.

Small holes in your skin help to keep your body at the right temperature. Tiny nerves send information to your brain about anything that you touch.

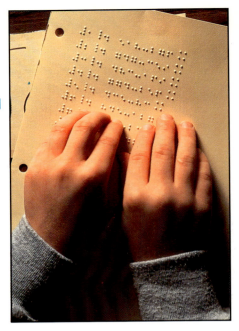

Braille is a way of printing letters as raised dots. Blind people can read Braille by feeling the dots with their fingers.

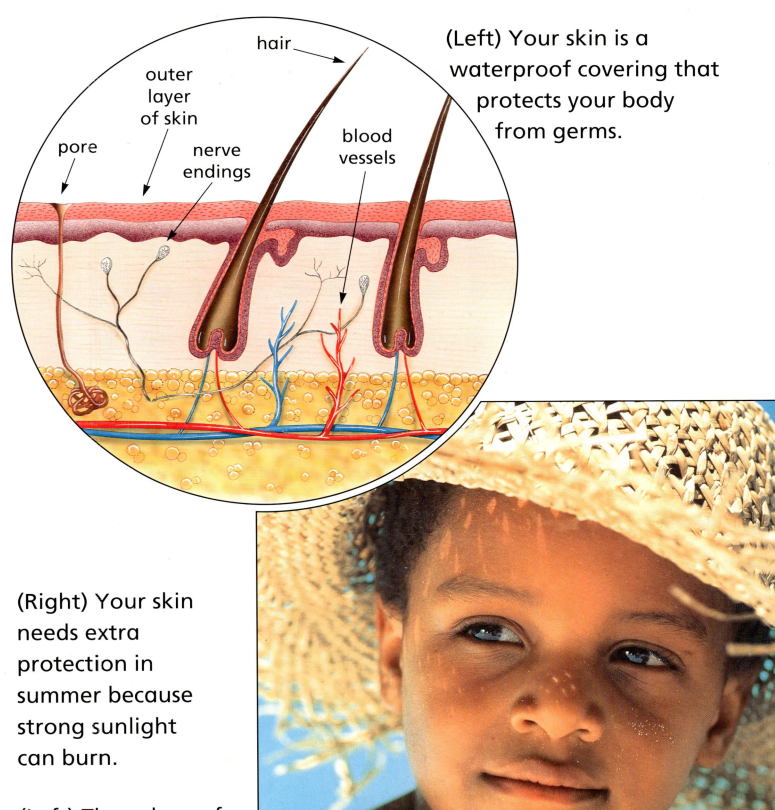

hair

outer
layer
of skin

pore

nerve
endings

blood
vessels

(Left) Your skin is a
waterproof covering that
protects your body
from germs.

(Right) Your skin
needs extra
protection in
summer because
strong sunlight
can burn.

(Left) The colour of
your skin depends on
the amount of
melanin you have.

Your Brain

Your brain looks after your whole body. It thinks for you, stores away your memories and keeps your body working the right way.

All parts of your body send messages to your brain through a thick nerve inside your backbone. Your brain then sends instructions back telling your body how to act.

Often your brain controls your actions without you knowing about them.

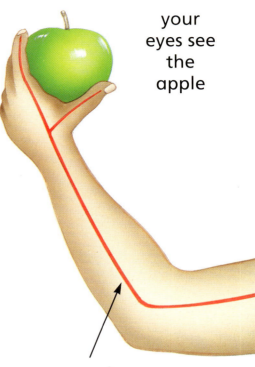

your eyes see the apple

nerves in your arm move your muscles

Your brain works hard when you are swimming. It tells your arms and legs how to move, makes sure you breathe at the right time and makes sure your muscles have enough energy.

16

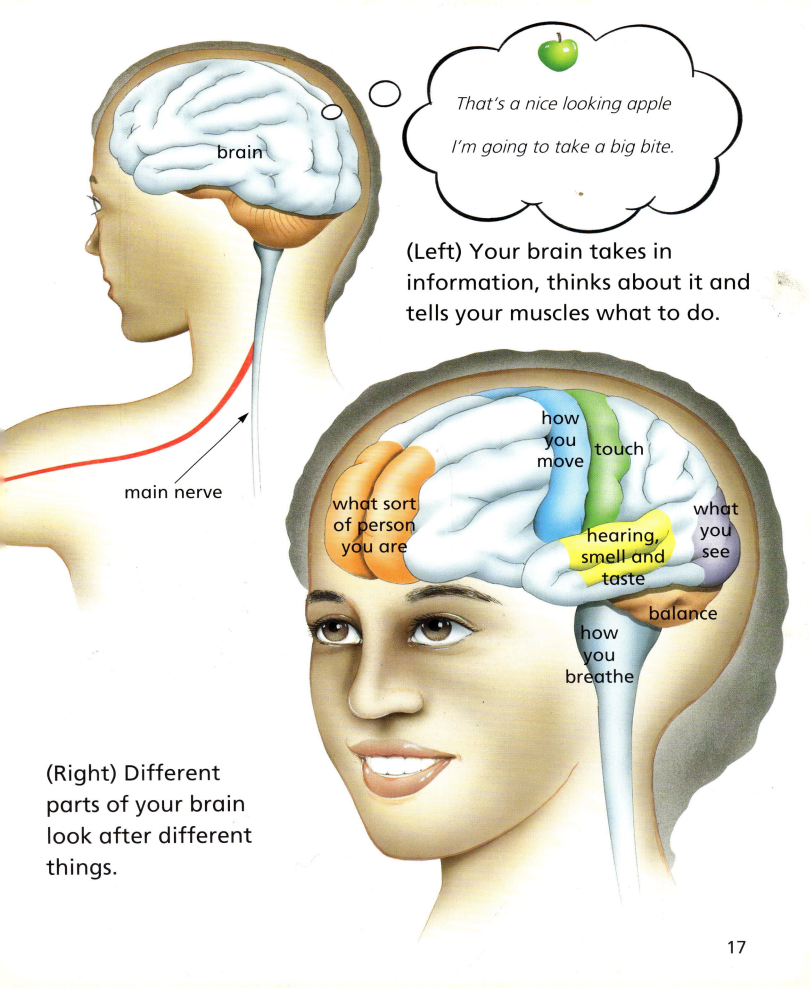

brain

That's a nice looking apple

I'm going to take a big bite.

(Left) Your brain takes in information, thinks about it and tells your muscles what to do.

main nerve

how you move

touch

what sort of person you are

hearing, smell and taste

what you see

balance

how you breathe

(Right) Different parts of your brain look after different things.

Seeing

Your eyes allow you to see the world around you.

The black parts at the centre are called pupils. In bright sunshine, your pupils are very small. These are the holes that let the light through to the back of your eyes. From here nerve cells send pictures to your brain.

Your eyelids and eyelashes help to protect your eyes from damage. Your tears wash them to keep them clean.

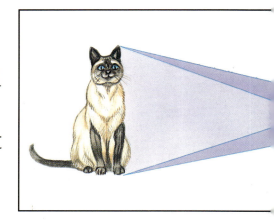

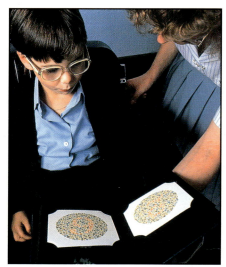

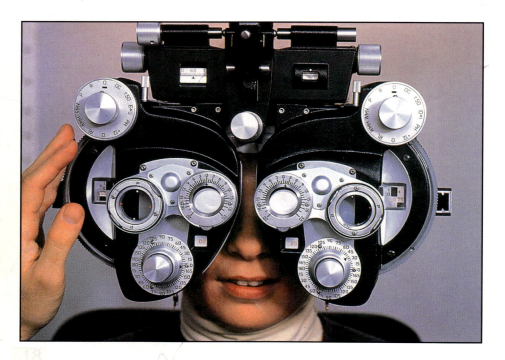

(Above) Some eye tests show how well you can see different colours.

(Left) Other tests show if you need to wear glasses.

Inside your eyes, pictures form
upside down on your retina.
Your brain sorts them out and
turns them the right way up.

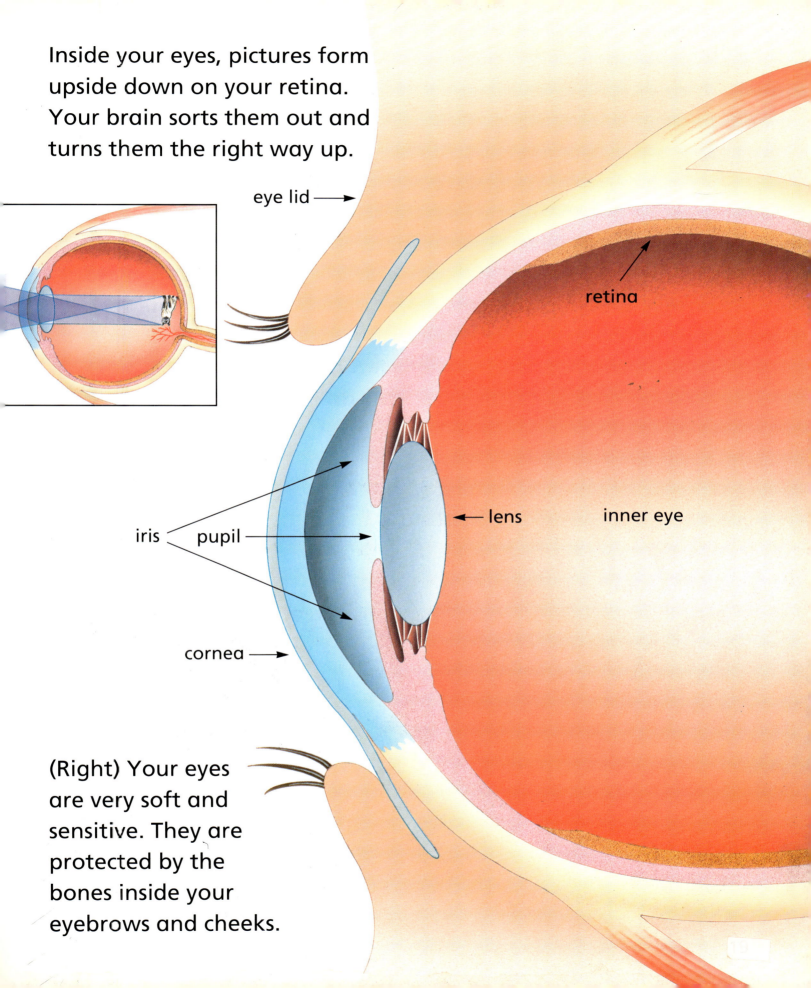

eye lid ⟶

retina

lens ⟵

inner eye

iris

pupil ⟶

cornea ⟶

(Right) Your eyes
are very soft and
sensitive. They are
protected by the
bones inside your
eyebrows and cheeks.

Hearing

The outer parts of your ears collect sounds from all around you and funnel them into the inner parts of your ears.

Inside, the sounds make your eardrums vibrate and small nerves send information about the sounds to your brain.

Your brain stores information about new sounds so you can recognize similar sounds when you hear them.

(Below) The cochlea receives vibrations from the stirrup and changes them into nerve signals which it sends to the brain.

cochlea

(Left) One part of your ear helps you to balance. If this part goes wrong, you will fall over when you try to walk.

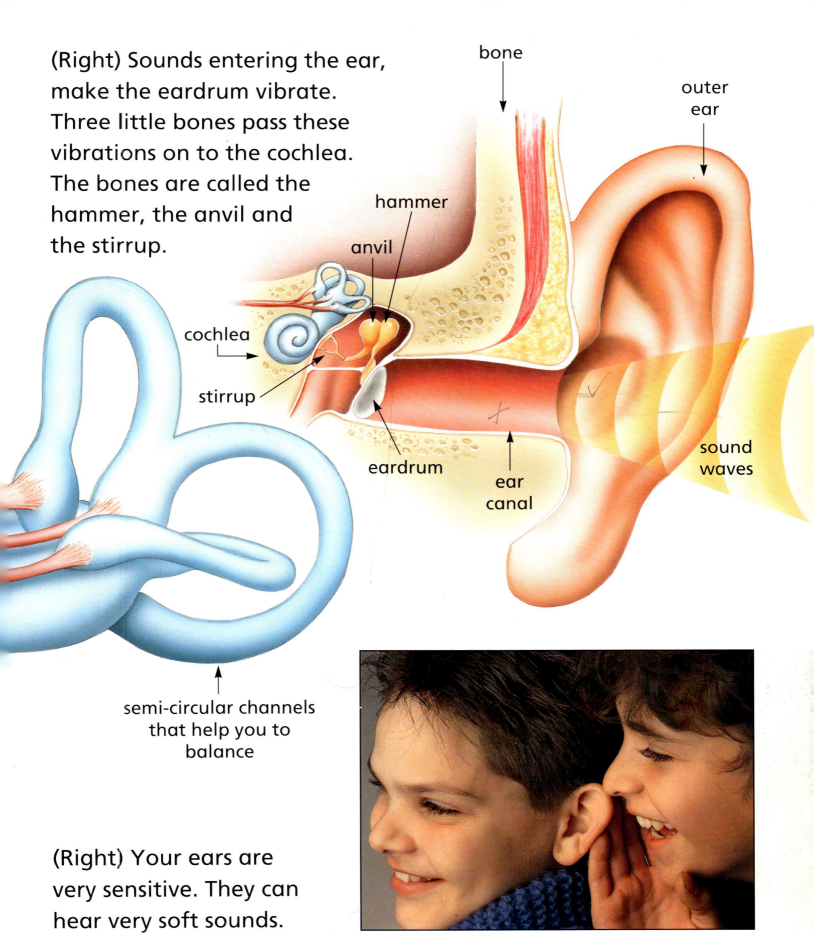

(Right) Sounds entering the ear, make the eardrum vibrate. Three little bones pass these vibrations on to the cochlea. The bones are called the hammer, the anvil and the stirrup.

bone

outer ear

hammer

anvil

cochlea

stirrup

eardrum

ear canal

sound waves

semi-circular channels that help you to balance

(Right) Your ears are very sensitive. They can hear very soft sounds.

Breathing

The air that you breathe in through your nose and mouth, moves down your windpipe and into your lungs. Inside your lungs, oxygen in the air can move into your blood.

Your brain controls your breathing all the time. When you sleep your breathing is slow, but when you run fast, you start to breathe more quickly.

Even when you are eating or drinking, air can still travel to your lungs.

When you run, you breathe quickly.

When you are asleep your breathing is slow.

When you breathe, air travels in through your nose, down your windpipe and into your lungs.

nerves sense smells

Small nerves at the top of your nose, sense any smells in the air and send the information to your brain.

← windpipe

← lung

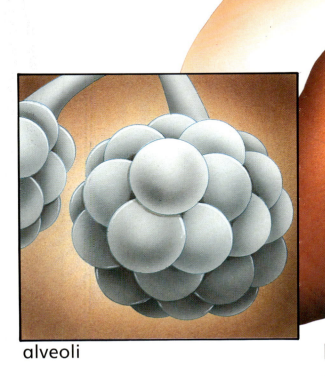

alveoli

Inside your lungs there are millions of tiny air sacs called alveoli.

Your Teeth

Your teeth are made of a hard bony material called dentine. The outside is protected by a thin layer of enamel and inside a soft core contains nerves and blood vessels. Different shapes of teeth have different jobs to do.

At about the age of 6, you begin to lose the milk teeth that grew when you were a baby. Your milk teeth are pushed out by new teeth growing underneath. By the age of 12, you will probably have almost a full set of teeth.

(Below left) Your back teeth are called molars. You use them for chewing. A molar has a double root inside your gum.

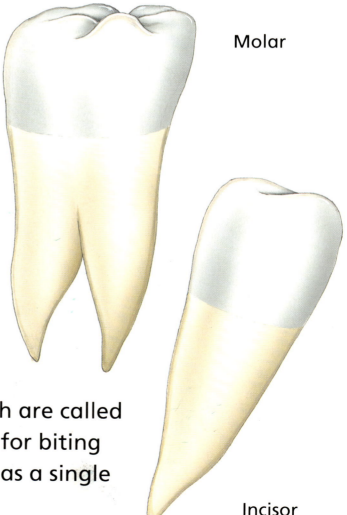

Molar

Incisor

(Right) Your front teeth are called incisors. You use them for biting your food. An incisor has a single root inside your gum.

(Left) Sleep rests your body and allows it to recharge like a battery.

(Right) Keeping your body clean keeps it healthy.

(Below) Eating healthy food makes sure that you have plenty of energy and that your body can grow and repair itself.

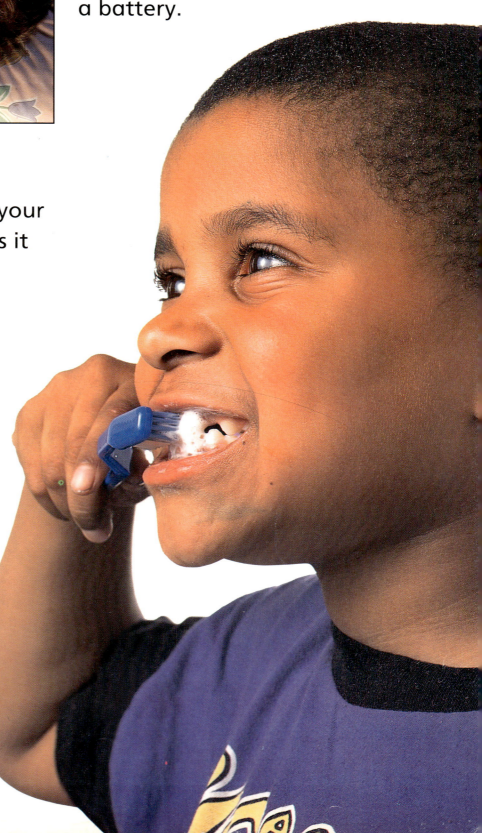

Word List

Arteries Tubes carrying your blood away from your heart to other parts of your body.

Blood group A way of naming different types of blood. Groups are A, B, AB and O.

Blood vessels Tubes inside your body that carry blood.

Cartilage Tough, flexible tissue attached to your bones.

Cell A very tiny part of a living creature. The smallest part of any living thing that can survive on its own.

Circulation The continuous movement of blood around your body.

Energy The store of strength that you have for action – walking, running and so on.

Food pipe A pipe that allows food to pass from your mouth to your stomach.

Germs Very tiny forms of life that can make you ill.

Heart beat The regular beat of your blood as your heart pumps it round your body. The rate of the beat is known as your pulse.

Infection A disease which can spread from person to person.

Intestines The long tube that carries liquids away from your stomach.

Lens The lens in your eye focuses light to give a clear picture.

Lungs Areas of spongy flesh inside your chest which let oxygen pass into your blood.

Melanin A substance that affects the colour of your skin and protects it from strong sunlight.

Microscope A machine through which you can see very small objects.

Muscles Groups of threads inside your body which can expand and contract like elastic.

Nerve A long thread that carries messages between your brain and other parts of your body so that your body can feel and move.

Oxygen A gas in the air which we need to breathe to keep us alive.

Veins Tubes that carry blood back to your heart.

Windpipe The tube through which air reaches the lungs.

Finding Out More

Places to Visit

The Science Museum,
Exhibition Road,
South Kensington,
London SW7.

The Natural History
Museum, Cromwell Rd;
London SW7 5BD.
The Human Biology
exhibition of the British
Museum (Natural
History) has a section on
'Growing'.

The Operating Theatre
Museum and Herb Garret,
9A St. Thomas' Street,
Southwark,
London SE1.

Books to Read

My Book About the Body,
Wayne Jackman (Wayland,
1991)

*Outside-In: (a lift-the-flap
body book)*, Clare Smallman
(Frances Lincoln, 1986)

*Inside Story: Read All
About Your Body*, Mike
Lambourne (Cassell, 1991)

What's Inside You?,
Susan Meredith (Usborne,
1991)

Look After Yourself:
a series of books including
*Stay Safe, Healthy Food,
Keep Clean!, Stay Fit!*
(Wayland, 1993)

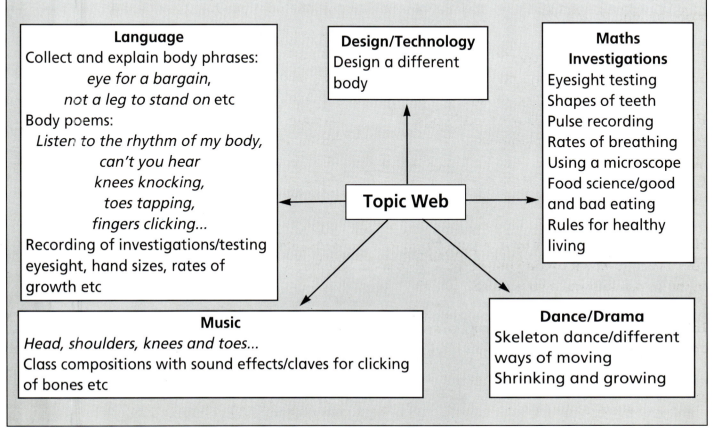

Language
Collect and explain body phrases:
*eye for a bargain,
not a leg to stand on* etc
Body poems:
*Listen to the rhythm of my body,
can't you hear
knees knocking,
toes tapping,
fingers clicking...*
Recording of investigations/testing
eyesight, hand sizes, rates of
growth etc

Design/Technology
Design a different
body

**Maths
Investigations**
Eyesight testing
Shapes of teeth
Pulse recording
Rates of breathing
Using a microscope
Food science/good
and bad eating
Rules for healthy
living

Topic Web

Music
Head, shoulders, knees and toes...
Class compositions with sound effects/claves for clicking
of bones etc

Dance/Drama
Skeleton dance/different
ways of moving
Shrinking and growing

Index